A Look at Canada

by Helen Frost

Consulting Editor: Gail Saunders-Smith, Ph.D.

Consultant: Barry G. Ferguson, Ph.D.
Professor of History
University of Manitoba
Winnipeg, Canada

Pebble Books

an imprint of Capstone Press
Mankato, Minnesota

Pebble Books are published by Capstone Press
151 Good Counsel Drive, P.O. Box 669, Mankato, Minnesota 56002
http://www.capstone-press.com

1 2 3 4 5 6 07 06 05 04 03 02

Library of Congress Cataloging-in-Publication Data
Frost, Helen, 1949–
    A look at Canada / by Helen Frost.
    p. cm.—(Our world)
    Includes bibliographical references and index.
    Summary: Simple text and photographs depict the land, animals, and people
of Canada.
    ISBN 0-7368-1166-4
    1. Canada—Juvenile literature. [1. Canada.] I. Title. II. Series.
F1008.2 .F76 2002
971—dc21   2001004829

Pebble Books thanks Natalie Johnson, M.A., Assistant to the Director, Institute for the
Humanities, University of Manitoba, for her assistance with this book. The author
thanks the children's section staff at Allen County Public Library in Fort Wayne,
Indiana, for research assistance.

Note to Parents and Teachers

The Our World series supports national social studies standards related to culture. This book describes and illustrates the land, animals, and people of Canada. The photographs support early readers in understanding the text. The repetition of words and phrases helps early readers learn new words. This book also introduces early readers to subject-specific vocabulary words, which are defined in the Words to Know section. Early readers may need assistance to read some words and to use the Table of Contents, Words to Know, Read More, Internet Sites, and Index/Word List sections of the book.

Table of Contents

Canada

Ottawa

★

Canada is in North America. Canada is the second largest country in the world. The capital of Canada is Ottawa.

mountain

forest

plains

tundra

6

Mountains, forests, and plains cover southern Canada. Frozen land called tundra is in northern Canada. This area is very cold in winter.

polar bear

Canada goose

Polar bears and caribou
live on the tundra. Canada
geese and loons spend
the summer in Canada.

More than 30 million people live in Canada. Most people live in cities in southern Canada. The country's largest cities are Toronto and Montreal.

English and French are
the official languages
of Canada. Students learn
to speak both languages.
Many Canadians also
speak other languages.

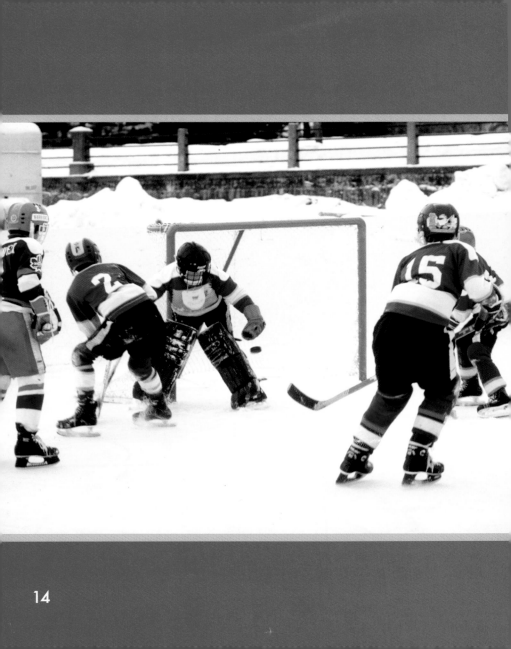

Canadians invented
ice hockey. This game
is Canada's most popular
sport. Many Canadians also
like to ski, boat, and camp.

Farmers in Canada grow wheat and potatoes to earn money. Workers make cars and newsprint. Many Canadians work in offices.

Canada's money is counted in Canadian dollars.

Canadians travel by train, car, and airplane. Some people travel by boat or snowmobile.

Maple trees grow in Canada. The maple leaf is a symbol of Canada. The Canadian flag has a red maple leaf on it.

Canada's flag

Words to Know

Canada goose—a common wild goose; Canada geese are gray with a black neck and head and a white patch on their face.

caribou—a large North American mammal that looks like a deer

hockey—a game played on ice with a stick and a puck; hockey players try to shoot the puck into a net.

maple leaf—a leaf that has five points; the sap from maple trees is good for making sugar and syrup; maple leaves turn red and orange in the fall.

polar bear—a large bear with thick, white fur; polar bears live in Arctic regions.

snowmobile—a vehicle with an engine and skis or runners; snowmobiles travel over snow.

symbol—an object that stands for something else

tundra—a large plain that is frozen most of the year; no trees grow on the tundra.

Read More

Gresko, Marcia S. *Canada*. Letters Home From. Woodbridge, Conn.: Blackbirch Press, 2000.

Hamilton, Janice. *A Ticket to Canada*. Minneapolis: Carolrhoda Books, 1999.

Landau, Elaine. *Canada*. A True Book. New York: Children's Press, 2000.

Meister, Cari. *Canada*. Going Places. Edina, Minn.: Abdo and Daughters, 2000.

Internet Sites

Canada Geography
http://www.photius.com/wfb2000/countries/canada/canada_geography.html

Geobop's Canada
http://www.geobop.com/world/na/canada

Teaching and Learning about Canada
http://www.canadainfolink.ca

Zoom School: Canada
http://www.enchantedlearning.com/school/Canada

Index/Word List

Word Count: 180
Early-Intervention Level: 17

Editorial Credits

Mari C. Schuh, editor; Kia Bielke, cover designer; Jennifer Schonborn, interior
illustrator and production designer; Kimberly Danger and Alta Schaffer,
photo researchers

Photo Credits

Canadian Tourism Commission, cover, 12, 14
Heather Robertson/Photo Agora, 6 (lower left)
One Mile Up, Inc., 21
Photo Network/Howard Folsom, 8 (top); Mark Newman, 8 (bottom)
Pictor/Mike Perry, 10; Randa Bishop, 18
Robert McCaw, 16
Unicorn Stock Photos/Aneal Vohra, 1; Richard B. Dippold, 20
Visuals Unlimited/Beth Davidow, 6 (upper left); D. Cavagnaro, 6 (upper right);
John Serrao, 6 (lower right)